D0476019

Published in 2017
by Autumn Publishing
Cottage Farm
Sywell
NN6 0BJ
www.igloobooks.com



LEO002 0517
2 4 6 8 10 9 7 5 3 1
ISBN 978-1-78810-666-5

The publisher would like to thank Alamy for permission to use the following image: pages 12–13 (centre), Zoonar GmbH / Alamy Stock Photo. All other images provided by iStockphoto.com.

Cover designed by Richard Sykes
Interiors designed by Starry Dog Books

Printed and manufactured in China

# 100

## FACTS FOR KIDS

# HUMAN BODY

# Parts of the Body

**FACT 1** Humans are mammals, like cats or horses. All mammals have hair, and the babies drink their mother's milk.

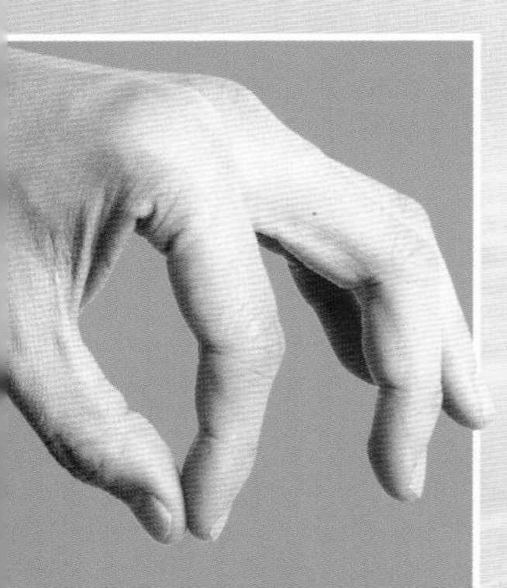

Gripping

**FACT 2** Most mammals have hair all over their bodies, but humans only have thick hair in a few places. Nobody really knows why!

**FACT 3** The middle of your body is called your torso. Inside it are organs that keep your body working.

**FACT 4** Your thumb and fingers can grip things. The only other animals that can do this are our relatives, monkeys and apes.

Leg

**FACT 5** Humans walk on two legs, unlike most mammals, which walk on four.

**FACT 6** Your head contains your brain, the most important part of your body.

**FACT 7** Human hands are perfect for holding things and making delicate movements.

**Torso**

**Head**

**Hand**

**FACT 8** Every part of your body is made up of tiny sections called cells.

**FACT 9** There are about 37 trillion (that's 37,000,000,000,000) cells in a human body.

**Inside a cell**

# Senses

**FACT 10** You find out about the world using your five senses: sight, smell, sound, touch and taste.

**FACT 11** Your sense of touch tells you when things are hot or cold, or when something is pushing or pulling against you.

**FACT 12** Tiny taste buds on your tongue work with your brain to tell you what something tastes like.

**FACT 13** The black circle in the middle of your eye is a hole called the pupil. Light passes through it into your eye.

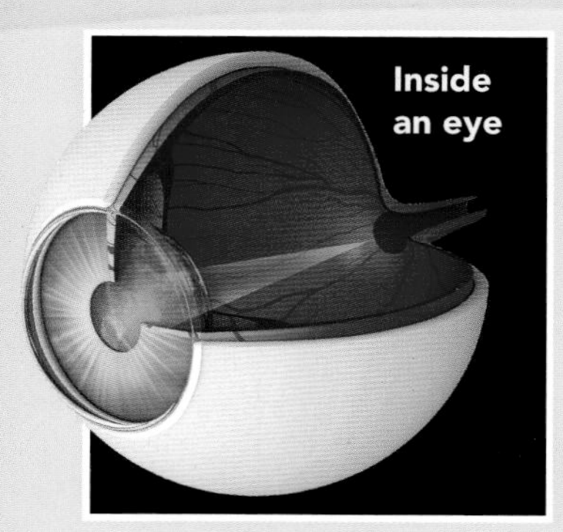

**Inside an eye**

**Hearing and touching**

**FACT 14** Your eyes detect light bouncing off things or shining out of them.

**FACT 15** The outside part of your ear acts like a radar dish, gathering sounds from around you.

Inside an ear

**FACT 16** The hole in your ear leads to your eardrum, a thin sheet of skin that detects sounds.

**FACT 17** Your nose can recognise millions of different smells.

Inside a nose

**FACT 18** Rotting food smells bad. Your nose and brain work together to warn you not to eat it.

# Skin, Hair and Nails

FACT 19 Skin is the largest of your body's organs. It covers you from head to toe and protects your insides.

FACT 20 Skin stops the fragile organs inside your body from drying out, and protects them from bumps.

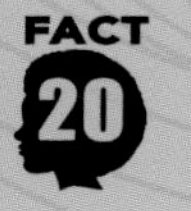

FACT 21 Your skin releases tiny amounts of oil. This keeps it soft and flexible.

Skin and hairs

FACT 22 When you get hot, your skin makes sweat: drops of water that cool you down as they dry.

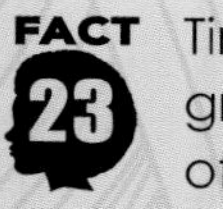

FACT 23 Tiny hairs grow on most of your body, but they are so thin they are hard to see.

FACT 24 The hairs on your head are about 0.1 mm (0.004 in) wide.

Sweat

FACT 25 An individual hair grows for 2 to 6 years before falling out.

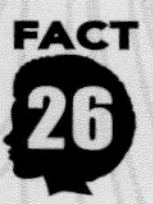

FACT 26 Most people have about 120,000 hairs on their heads.

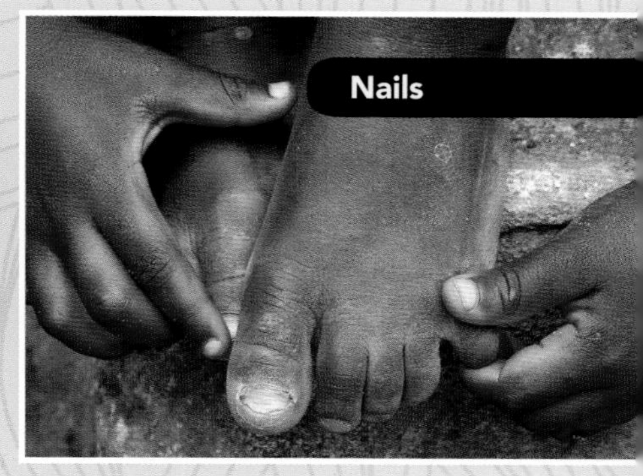

Nails

FACT 27 Your fingernails and toenails are made of the same stuff as rhino horn.

FACT 28 Fingernails grow about twice as fast as toenails.

# Bones

**FACT 29** Your skeleton holds your body up and protects important organs, such as your brain and heart.

**FACT 30** When you are born you have 270 bones. As you grow up, some join together. Adults only have 206 bones.

**FACT 31** Your backbone, or spine, holds you upright. It is made up of 33 little bones called vertebrae.

**FACT 32** Squidgy discs sit between your vertebrae to stop them rubbing together.

Skeleton

Backbone

Backbone

Skull

Your head is protected by your bony skull, which keeps your brain safe.

There are 22 bones in your skull.

Your bones are made of a hard outside and a spongy inside.

The big bones in your body are filled with marrow. Blood cells grow inside the marrow.

Inside a bone

**FACT 37** The ends of your bones are protected by a rubbery coating called cartilage, which stops them grinding together.

# Brain and Nerves

**FACT 38** Your brain is where all your thoughts and feelings happen, and where your memories are stored.

**FACT 39** Different parts of your brain control different things. One part controls memory, another part controls speaking, and so on.

Brain

**FACT 40** Humans have very large brains for our size. This makes us smarter than other animals.

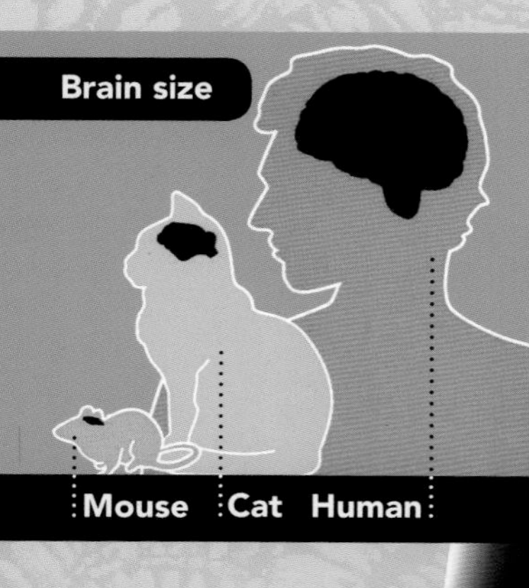

FACT 41 Nerves are threads that carry messages to and from your brain.

FACT 42 Nerves tell your brain what your body is feeling, for example when you are hot, cold, hungry or ticklish.

FACT 43 Your fingers have lots of nerves. This makes them very good at feeling things.

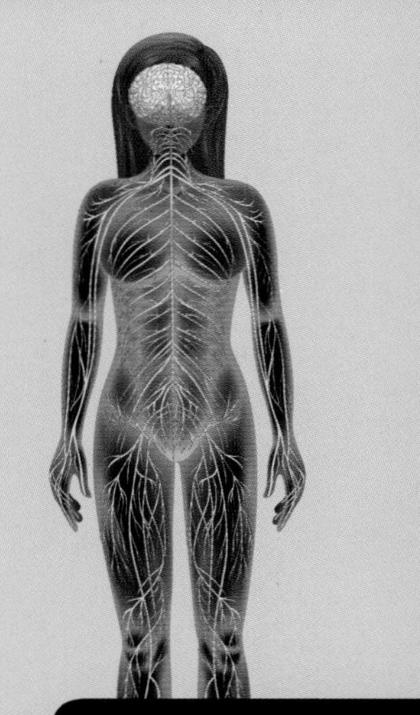
Nervous system

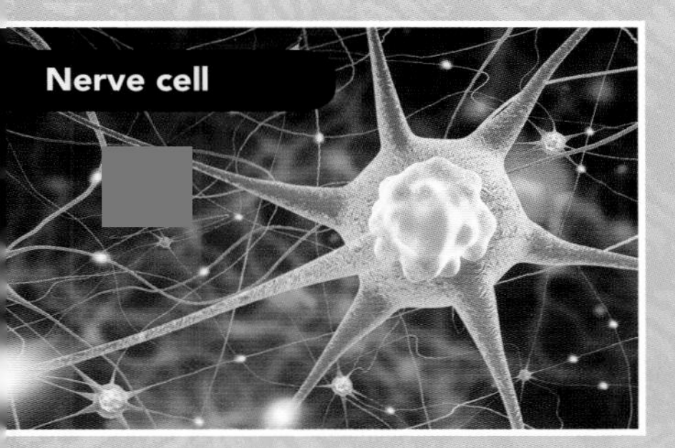
Nerve cell

FACT 44 Nerves also send messages from your brain to parts of your body, telling them when to move or work.

FACT 45 Your nerves use tiny amounts of electricity to send signals, like wires in a computer.

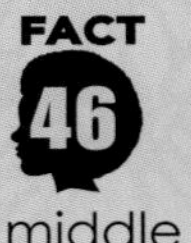
FACT 46 A bundle of nerves called your spinal cord runs down the middle of your backbone.


Spinal column

# Digestion

FACT 47 When you eat, your body turns food into energy you can use to grow and move. This process is called digestion.

Stomach

Eating

Your mouth is like a food processor. Your teeth mash up food and mix it with saliva to make a soft paste.

FACT 49 When you swallow, your tongue pushes food down a long tube towards your stomach.

FACT 50 Strong acid in your stomach breaks the food down into fuel that your body can use.

FACT 51

After leaving your stomach, food travels along two long, looping tubes called your intestines.

Food passes through your small intestine first. Then it goes into your large intestine, which is shorter but wider.

Your intestines are lined with tiny hair-shaped cells that soak up useful bits of food and leave the rest.

Large intestine

Unused food passes through your large intestine and leaves your body as faeces (poo).

FACT 55

It takes about 8 hours for food to go from your mouth to your small intestine. Then it can take another 40 hours for food to pass through your intestines and out of your body.

# Other Organs

**FACT 56** Your body has special organs to keep it healthy and get rid of rubbish and poisons.

**FACT 57** Your kidneys clean your blood. They take out rubbish and extra water and turn them into urine (wee).

**FACT 58** A human liver weighs about 1.5 kg (3 lb), or the same as a large bottle of water.

**FACT 59** Your liver keeps your insides clean. It soaks up poisonous chemicals and turns them into harmless ones.

**Liver**

**FACT 60** Your liver does about 500 different jobs, including storing energy and fighting diseases.

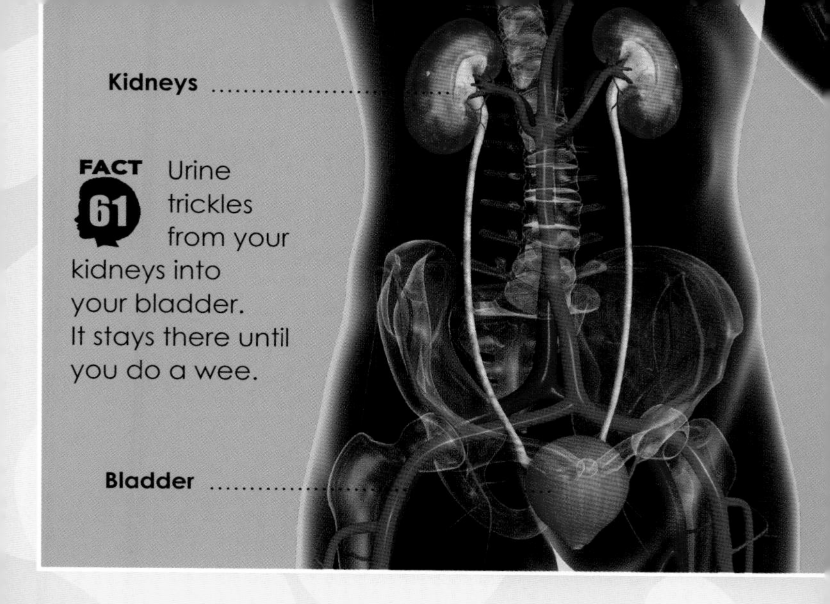


**FACT 61** Urine trickles from your kidneys into your bladder. It stays there until you do a wee.

**FACT 62** Your bladder is stretchy. It's about the size of a golf ball when it's empty, but the size of a large orange when it's full.

**FACT 63** A small organ called the pancreas helps your intestines to digest food.

**FACT 64** The pancreas also looks after your energy levels by controlling the amount of sugar in your blood.

Pancreas

# Muscles

**FACT 65** Muscles are what make your body move. You have more than 650 muscles altogether.

**FACT 66** Muscles are made of tiny threads called fibres. They stretch and pull like strings of elastic.

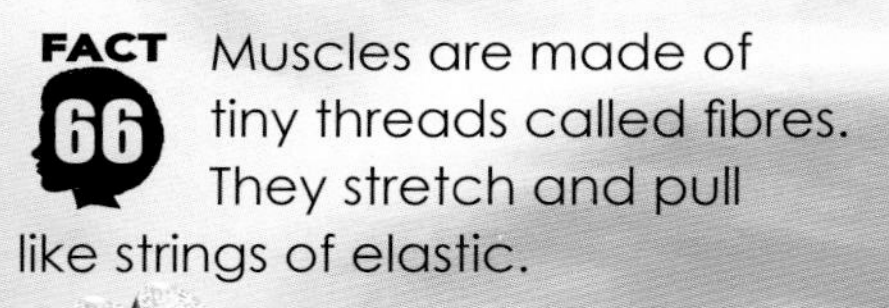

Muscle fibres

**FACT 67** Your knees and elbows are joints, or hinges where two bones meet.

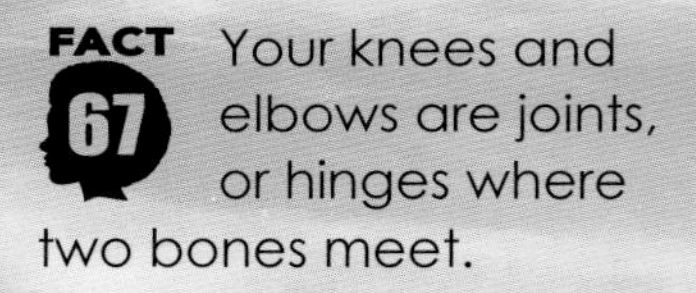

**FACT 68** Muscles in your arms and legs pull against the bones to make them move.

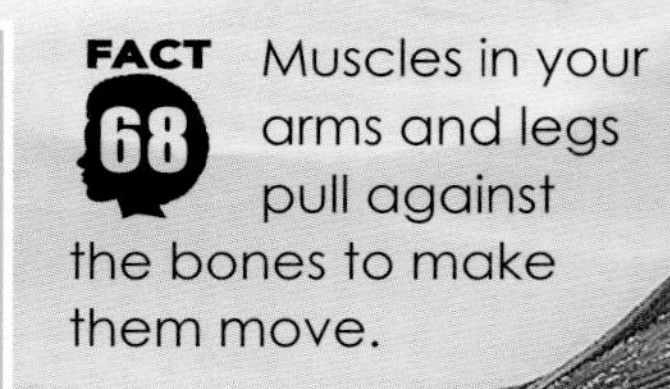

Elbow joint

Muscles

Exercise

FACT 69 Muscles get stronger the more they are used. Exercise keeps them strong and healthy.

FACT 70 You use muscles in your eyes to look around.

Muscle system

FACT 71 Muscles in your intestines move food along.

FACT 72 The biggest muscles in your body are in your bottom, back and legs. You use them to stay upright, walk and run.

# Heart and Lungs

**FACT 73** To stay alive, your body needs to breathe in fresh air and blow out used air.

**Blowing out used air**

**FACT 74** Your lungs are big air bags in your chest. They fill up to take in new air, and squish down to blow out used air.

**FACT 75** Air contains a gas called oxygen that your body needs to survive. Your lungs soak up oxygen from the air.

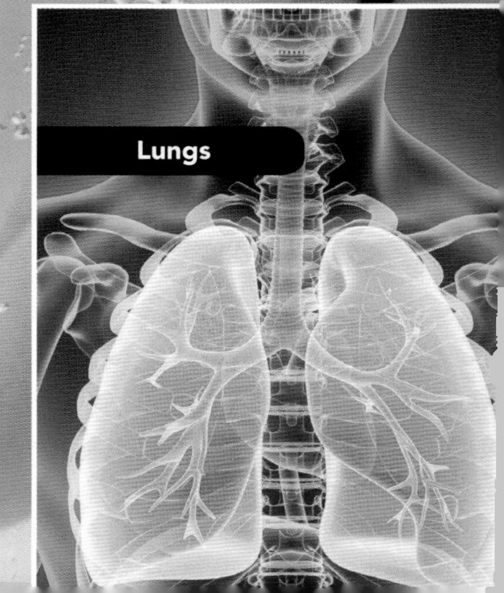

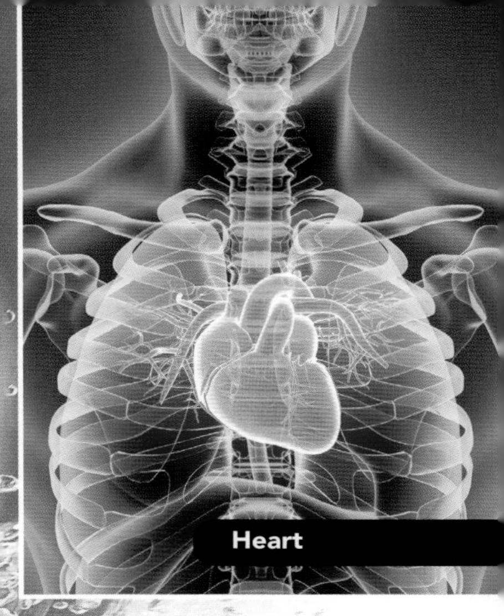


FACT 76 Your heart is a powerful pump that sends blood all around your body.

FACT 77 If you put your head against a person's chest, you can hear their heart beating.

FACT 78 Your heart is about the same size as your fist.

FACT 79 An adult's heart beats about once every second when resting. Children's hearts beat faster.

FACT 80 Every year your heart beats more than 40 million times!

FACT 81 When you exercise, your heart beats faster, as your body needs more oxygen to keep moving.

# Blood and Blood Vessels

**FACT 82** Blood is a red liquid that flows all around your body. It carries energy and water to every cell.

**FACT 83** Blood is a mixture of lots of different things floating in a watery goo called plasma.

**FACT 84** Your blood takes rubbish away from your cells and carries it to your liver and kidneys for cleaning.

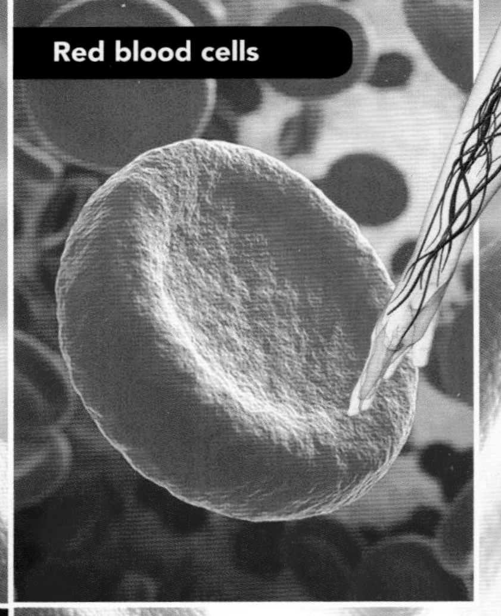

Red blood cells

White blood cell

**FACT 85** Red blood cells float around in your blood. They carry oxygen around your body.

**FACT 86** White blood cells are bigger than red blood cells. Their job is to hunt down germs in your blood and destroy them.

**FACT 87** Blood flows all around your body in tubes called blood vessels.

**FACT 88** The widest blood vessel is about 2 cm (1 in) across. The smallest is thinner than a hair.

**FACT 89** Veins are blood vessels that carry blood towards your heart. Arteries carry blood away from your heart.

**FACT 90** Most people have about 5 litres (9 pints) of blood in their body.

**Blood vessels and heart**

# Staying Healthy

To stay healthy, you need to look after your amazing body.

Exercise

Exercising keeps your body fit and strong. Running around makes your heart beat faster, which helps it to stay healthy.

Your body needs to eat the right kinds of food to make it work properly.

FACT 94

Fruit and vegetables contain vitamins that keep your body working well.

Fruit and vegetables

Germ

FACT 95 Germs are tiny creatures that can make you sick. They often live in dirt.

Water

FACT 96 If you do get sick, your body can make its own medicine. Special cells and chemicals kill germs inside your blood and organs.

FACT 97 Washing hands with soap kills germs and washes them away, so they can't hurt you.

FACT 98 Your body needs lots of water. You need to drink water every day so your organs can do their jobs.

# Growing Up

Babies grow inside their mothers. They start out as a single tiny cell.

It takes nine months for a single cell to grow into a baby that's ready to be born.

FACT 101 Your body makes special chemicals called hormones that help you to grow and develop.

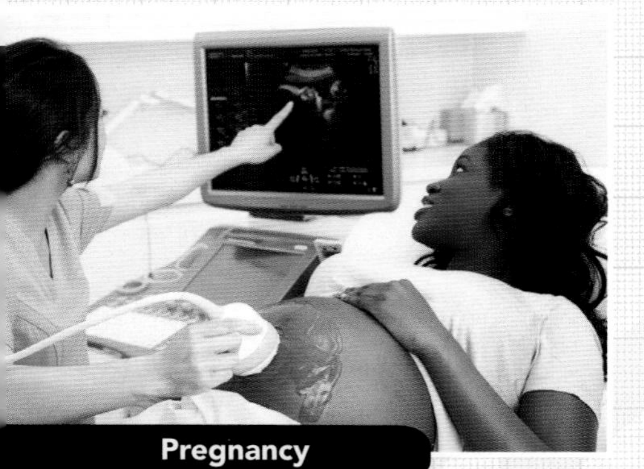

Pregnancy

**FACT 102** The tallest person ever was Robert Wadlow. He was 2.7 m (8.9 ft) tall.

Newborn baby

**FACT 103** Most newborn babies are about 50 cm (20 in) tall.

**FACT 104** When you are a teenager, your body changes from a child into an adult. This is called puberty.

**FACT 105** Most adults grow to be about 3.5 times taller and 18 times heavier than a newborn baby.